I0828200

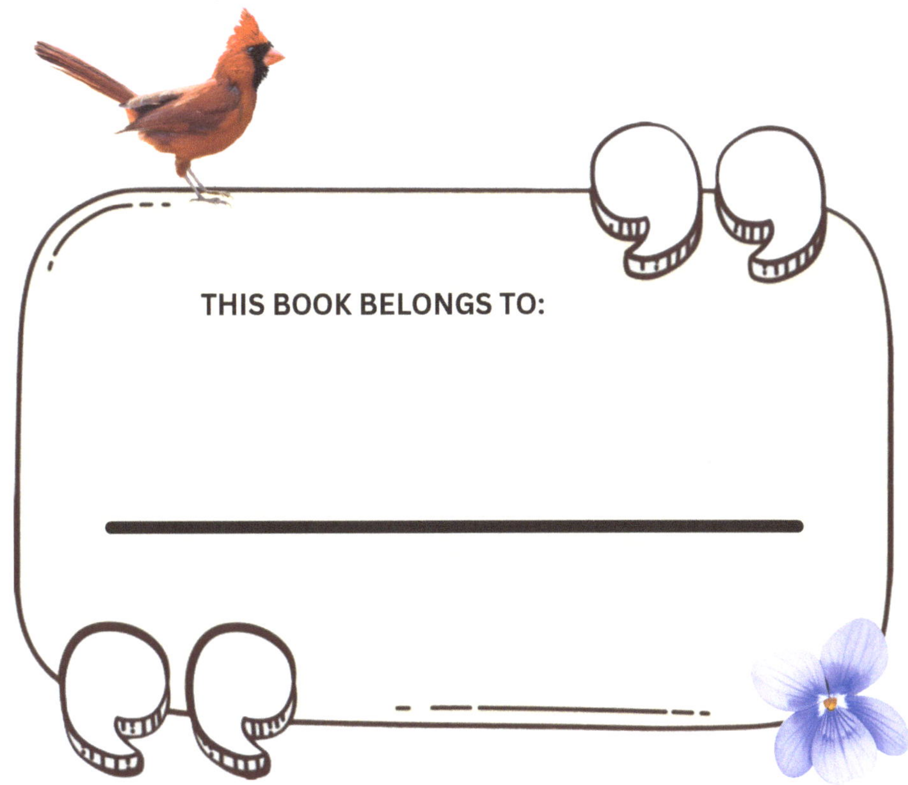
THIS BOOK BELONGS TO:

WELCOME TO ILLINOIS

Dedicated to all the explorers.

ISBN 978-1-958985-96-0

www.joeysavestheday.com

Mimi Books™ Publishing

A Mimi Book

Illinois got its name from the Illiniwek, a group of Native American tribes who lived in the region long before settlers arrived. Early French explorers wrote the name as "Illinois," adding a silent "s" at the end. The word is often said to mean "the people" or "the best people." Over time, the name Illinois became the official name of the state we know today.

Illinois has a long history that begins with Native American nations who lived along its rivers, forests, and prairies for thousands of years. Tribes such as the Illiniwek, Miami, and Potawatomi built strong communities across the region. In the 1600s, French explorers and traders arrived, followed later by settlers who established new towns and farms. As the population grew, Illinois became an important crossroads for travel, trade, and new communities.

Illinois was the twenty-first state to join the Union. It officially joined on December 3, 1818.

21st

Illinois is located in the Midwestern United States. It is bordered by Wisconsin, Iowa, Missouri, Kentucky, and Indiana, and it also touches Michigan across Lake Michigan.

Springfield is the capital of Illinois.
It officially became the capital in 1837.

Chicago, Illinois, has an estimated population of about 2.70 million people.

There are approximately 12,700,000 people residing in the state of Illinois.

Elgin, Illinois

Illinois is the twenty-fifth largest state in the United States by area.

Chicago, Illinois

ILLINOIS

There are 102 counties in Illinois.

Here is a list of twenty of those counties:

Adams
Alexander
Bond
Boone
Brown
Clinton
Coles
Cook
Crawford
Cumberland
Edwards
Effingham
Fayette
Ford
Franklin
Ogle
Peoria
Perry
Piatt
Pike

Abraham Lincoln, the 16th President of the United States, is remembered at Lincoln's Tomb in Oak Ridge Cemetery in Springfield, Illinois. The tall, shiny monument has a big stone tower and friendly bronze statues that help tell the story of the Civil War. Inside the tomb, Lincoln rests with his wife, Mary Todd Lincoln, and three of their sons.

Matthiessen State Park is one of Illinois' most beautiful nature spots, filled with tall cliffs, winding canyons, and peaceful forest trails. Its main waterfall, Cascade Falls, flows down into a cool, rocky canyon that was shaped by water over thousands of years. Kids can watch the water spill over the sandstone ledge and follow the stream as it twists through the canyon floor. In spring, the waterfall is lively and bright, and in winter, it can freeze into a sparkling ice column.

One of the most important moments in Illinois history is the opening of the Illinois and Michigan Canal in 1848. This long waterway connected the Great Lakes to the Mississippi River, allowing boats to travel from the East Coast all the way to the Gulf of Mexico. The canal helped small towns grow into busy communities and made Chicago an important center for trade and travel. Today, parts of the canal are preserved as a historic trail, reminding visitors how this major project helped shape Illinois and the entire country.

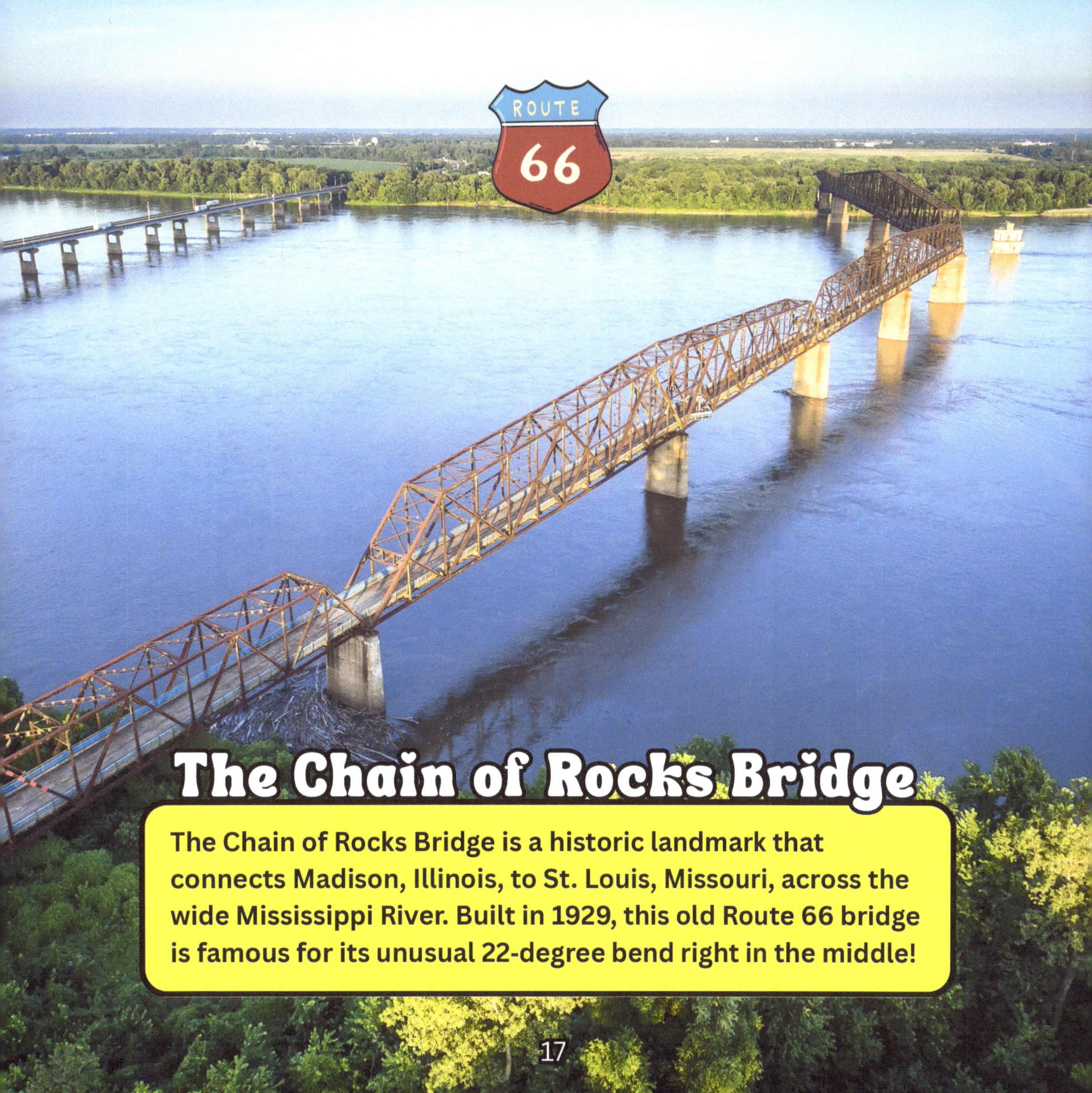

The Chain of Rocks Bridge

The Chain of Rocks Bridge is a historic landmark that connects Madison, Illinois, to St. Louis, Missouri, across the wide Mississippi River. Built in 1929, this old Route 66 bridge is famous for its unusual 22-degree bend right in the middle!

A couple of Illinois' nicknames include the Prairie State and the Land of Lincoln.

LAND

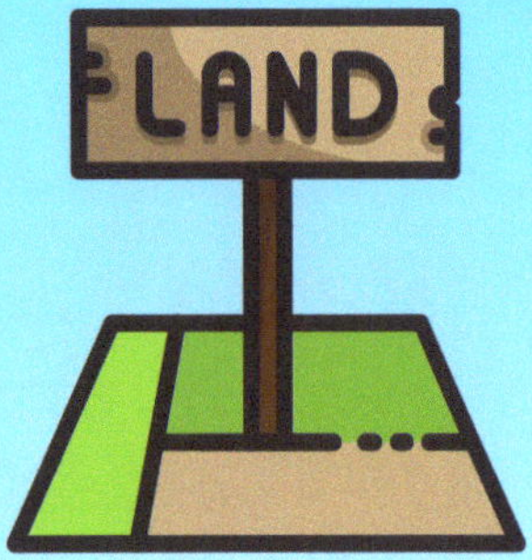

of

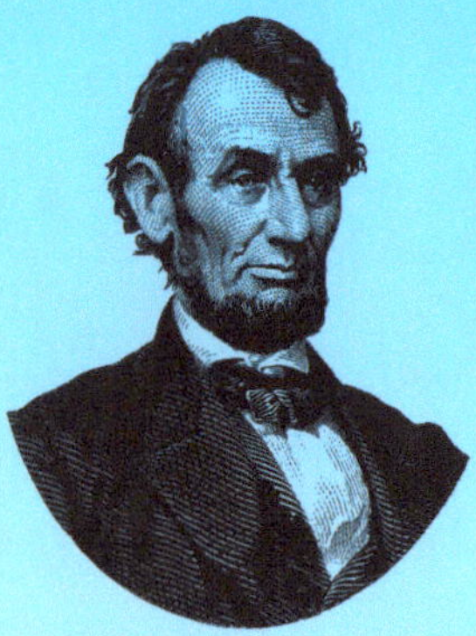

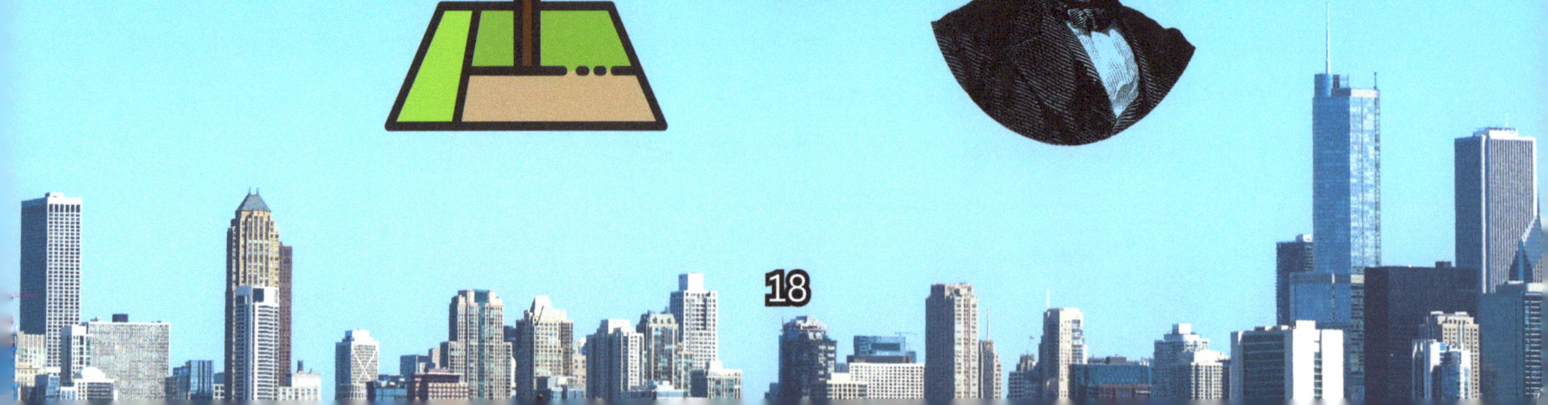

Illinois' state motto is "State Sovereignty, National Union." It was adopted in 1818.

What "State Sovereignty, National Union" Means:

- State Sovereignty means each state has the power to make its own laws and take care of its own needs.
- National Union means all the states are still part of one big country and work together as the United States.

Put together, the motto is saying:

Illinois believes in the rights of each state, while also believing in staying united as one nation.

ILLINOIS
ILLINOIS
ILLINOIS
ILLINOIS
The abbreviation for Illinois is IL.
IL

Illinois' state flag was officially adopted in 1915.

Some crops grown in Illinois are corn, soybeans, wheat, and pumpkins.

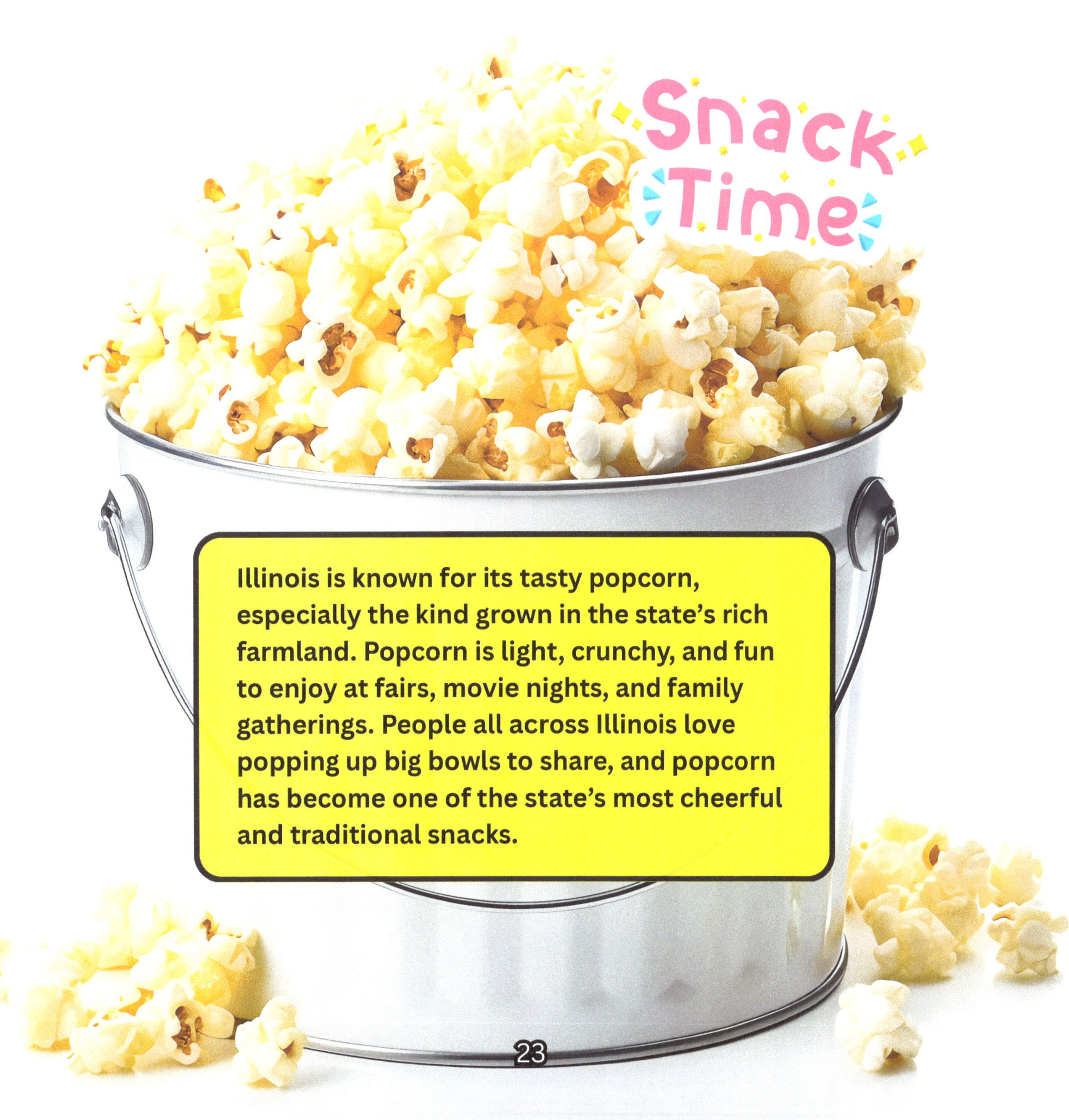

Illinois is known for its tasty popcorn, especially the kind grown in the state's rich farmland. Popcorn is light, crunchy, and fun to enjoy at fairs, movie nights, and family gatherings. People all across Illinois love popping up big bowls to share, and popcorn has become one of the state's most cheerful and traditional snacks.

Some animals that live in Illinois are white-tailed deer, red foxes, coyotes, raccoons, and eastern gray squirrels.

The Brookfield Zoo near Chicago is a wonderful place to explore, with animals from all around the world. Kids can see lions, bears, giraffes, dolphins, and playful primates, along with colorful birds and reptiles.

The Illinois state bird is the Northern Cardinal.
It was chosen as the state bird in 1929.

The bluegill is Illinois' state fish. It's a small, colorful fish with bright patterns and a round, friendly shape that make it easy to spot in ponds, lakes, and slow-moving rivers. The bluegill was officially adopted as the state fish in 1986.

Illinois experiences a wide range of temperatures throughout the year. The hottest temperature ever recorded in the state was 117 degrees Fahrenheit, measured in East St. Louis on July 14, 1954. In contrast, the coldest temperature documented was −38 degrees Fahrenheit, recorded in Mount Carroll on January 31, 2019.

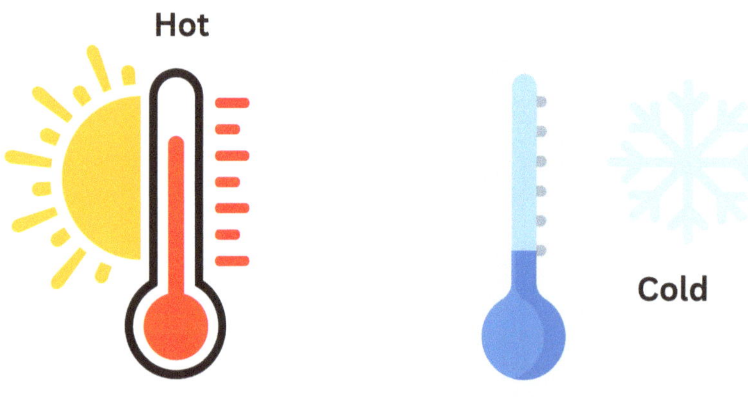

Ida B. Wells was a brave journalist who lived in Chicago. She spoke up for fairness and equal rights and worked hard to make her community better. People remember her for her courage and strong voice.

The largest airport in Illinois is O'Hare International Airport, located in Chicago. It sits at 10000 West O'Hare Avenue and serves as the main travel hub for people flying in and out of Illinois. This airport connects travelers to cities all across the country and to destinations around the world, making it one of the busiest and most important airports in the United States.

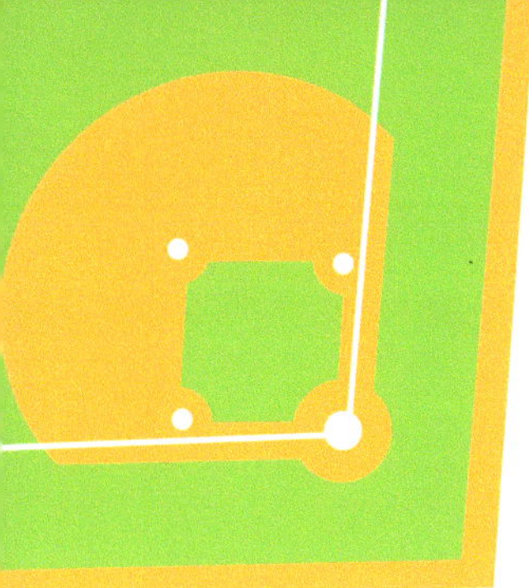

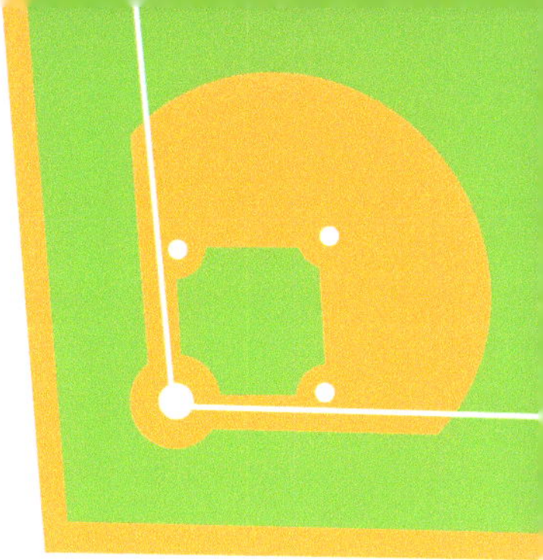

The Chicago Cubs are a Major League Baseball team based in Chicago, one of Illinois' most famous cities. They play their home games at Wrigley Field, a bright and lively ballpark known for its friendly atmosphere, historic charm, and iconic ivy-covered outfield walls. The Cubs are one of the oldest teams in baseball, and many talented players have worn their uniform as they built their skills and made baseball history.

FOOTBALL

The Chicago Bears are a major professional football team with a huge fan base all across Illinois, where many families cheer for them every season. The team plays its home games at Soldier Field in Chicago, a loud and energetic stadium filled with fans wearing navy blue and orange.

The official state flower of Illinois is the Violet. It was chosen as the state flower in 1908.

The white oak is Illinois' state tree. It's known for its strong branches and bright green leaves that turn shades of red and gold in the fall. The white oak was officially adopted as the state tree in 1908, and its sturdy, long-lasting wood has made it a beloved symbol of Illinois's natural beauty.

Can you name these?

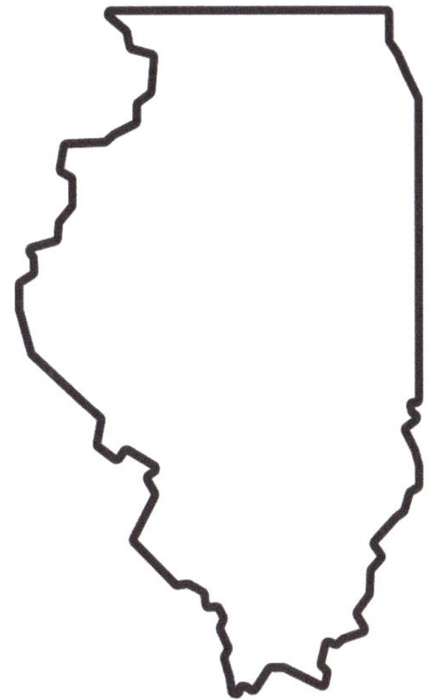

I hope you enjoyed learning about Illinois.

To explore fun facts about the other 49 states, visit my website at www.joeysavestheday.com. You'll also find a wide variety of homeschool resources to support joyful learning at home. If you enjoyed this book, I would be grateful if you left a review. Your feedback truly helps. Thank you for your support!

Check out these other interesting books in the 50 States Fact Books Series!

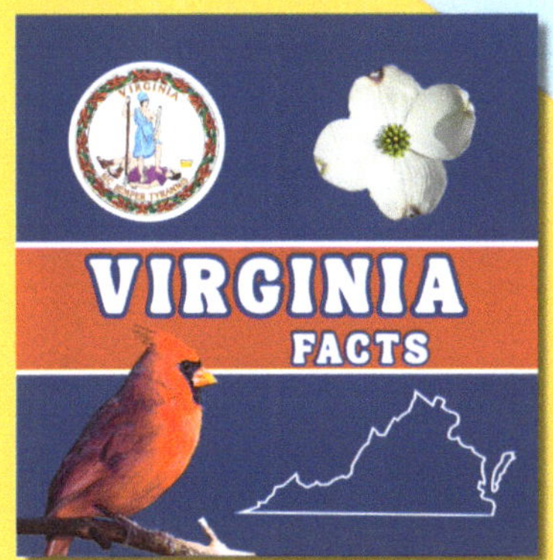

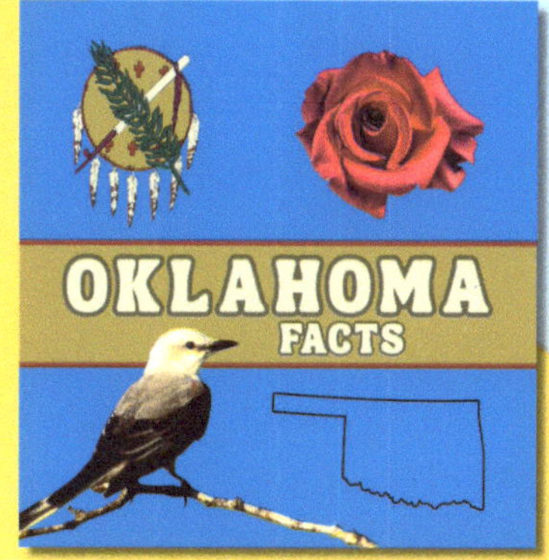

www.mimibooks.com